PHILosophies

PHIL M. JONES

Published by Philmjones Ltd

While the publisher has taken reasonable care in the preparation of this book, the publisher makes no representation, express or implied, with regard to the accuracy of the information contained in this book and cannot accept legal responsibility or liability for any errors or omissions from the book or the consequences thereof.

Products or services that are referred to in this book may be either trademarks and/or registered trademarks of their respective owners. The publishers and author make no claims to these trademarks.

A CIP Catalogue record for this book is available from the British Library.

The moral rights of the author have been asserted.

Design by www.ebook-designs.co.uk

Printed in Great Britain by Lulu

INTRODUCTION

The fact that you've picked this book up proves that you want more and are determined to find ways in order to make it happen.

I truly commend you.

What you truly desire is within reach and in this book, I want to help you make those dreams become a reality.

Over the coming pages, you're going to read 52 of my *"Philosophies"* – these are lessons, observations and bite-sized info that I've acquired throughout my career, speaking to tens of thousands of business owners, and working with many well-known companies.

I live my life based on these rules and if you want to not only grow your business but also improve your health, wealth and relationships; then I urge you to live & breath these "Philosophies" with me.

You can use them as motivation, inspiration or practical guidance to live your life by – but one thing's for sure – if you take my hand and start using these in your day-to-day life, you'll notice real changes to the way you think and the way you act.

Keep this book to hand, dip in when you feel the need and let's create a great future together.

Keep being brilliant.

philmjones
INTERNATIONAL
helping your business reach new heights

ABOUT THE
AUTHOR

Phil M Jones is an award-winning international speaker, author and trainer, having worked within more than fifty countries across five continents.

Highly recognised as the authority in worldwide sales psychology and negotiation, Phil works with both global companies to increase their profitability and with Network Marketers to increase their results generating more freedom.

This is Phil's third book, after previously writing two Amazon best-selling books including Toolbox and Magic Words.

To succeed is to start. If today you start more conversations than normal days, just then imagine what happens if you keep starting conversations.

It is trial and error and the important thing to think about is that being busy is what gets you busy.

When you start conversations, those conversations lead us to opportunity.

Not every conversation reaps the rewards you wish for. We must still keep at it and just like fishing, not every cast catches a fish but as you keep trying you keep learning.

Celebrate your progress, your ambition and your willingness to try. You are not like most people because you have already decided you want more.

You are awesome and I admire that. Many though, envy that. You are a champion and that means if you keep moving forward then you will win the race.

2

When you focus on the impossible, the difficult and the challenging you are faced with two choices.

1. Is to grow the obstacle bigger and tell yourself it's not achievable for you at this stage.

2. Is to grow yourself to rise over the obstacle and never let it worry you again.

The only difference between the 2 is the choice that you make.

The obstacle is always the same...

By trying, trying again and trying some more we reach a new level of mastery quicker than any other way.

Just wanted to remind you of some things you may have once thought were impossible or were for other people and not you...

- Walking
- Talking
- Tying your shoelaces
- Riding a bike
- Cooking a meal
- Swimming
- Driving a car

I mean I could write a list forever...

You have a proven track record of success, a proven track record of achievement and a victory journal to be proud of.

You are a human being and by being human you can overcome the most colossal of challenges.

Don't ever let someone tell you that you cannot do something.

Least of all yourself.

You have sowed the seeds of success and have created many a new customer and opened many new doors.

The seeds of success need to be continually nurtured and many will not sprout or grow at all.

You have no idea which ones will develop and which ones will fail. Your job is to water them all, take care of them all and then nourish the ones that start to sprout, cherish the ones that start to grow and protect the ones that bear the fruit.

This is your business and it is responsible for funding the life you dream of.

Don't ever let anyone else take that away from you!

For a plan to work in reality then it must always work on paper first.

Before you build a house you have an architect draw a plan;
Before you take a long drive you plan your route;
Before you set out on the Ikea flatpack you check the plan!

I find it crazy that most people spend more time planning a 2 week vacation, than they do their business and their future success.

Only once you have made a plan can you succeed. Because without knowing what success truly looks like you are a wandering existence.

If you fail to make a plan then you will soon become a part of someone else's!

In the words of Kevin Costner in the movie Field of Dreams. "Build it and they will come."

Understanding the numbers of your business may take time, yet I am certain they will help you build what you are looking for.

Success or failure, the one consistent is that everything else around you will happen regardless. If you want to see a change then you have to be that change!

Your future life is in your hands and the decisions, choices and actions that you make will provide you the exact outcome that you deserve.

The past is history and you are no longer who you were. Today is your moment to step up, reinvent and take a big step in the right direction.

It is important for you to know that in my life things have not been easy, in fact I have been faced with a truck load of adversity and had to overcome many a tough time.

During one particular tough time in my life I was driving late at night and just had to pull over because I knew I needed to make a change.

What flowed out of my pen that night was this poem. Written in one take and without an edit...

If life could be easier
I would have more of what I want
Enjoy all the things I love
And none of what I don't

If the economy was better
More cash would come my way
My accounts would look better
The pain would go away

If Lady Luck would visit
Good fortune shine on me
I could get what I deserve
Be all that I can be

If is just a question
The blame pointed elsewhere
Excuses and denial
In fact it's just not fair!

If I am to be successful
And have all I desire
At first I simply look inside
Pour fuel upon the fire

If I believe in myself
Be what I need to be
If someone else can do it
Can someone else be me?

If I'm prepared to take the action
Climb mountains on the way
Follow through, don't give up
Let nothing get in my way

If success is what I am after
I must take responsibility
Everything that happens
Is accountable to me

I can have what I want
Live everything I dream
Feel happy and contented
Be that cat that got the cream

If everything was easy
Just handed on a plate
Would success be worth it?
Would life be so great?

If life is but a journey
I will plan it carefully
Live for every moment
Be what I can be

If I just stay focussed
Each day commit and do
Great things will start to happen
They're happening to you

If it is really worth it
What difference could I make
Stand up and just be counted
Be more and don't be fake

If is just a question
Success is by design
I know what I am doing
Things will be just fine...

If I take control
Target on the result
Success will come my way
Success is all my fault

7

Perhaps the most important quality one can have is the ability to change, adapt and evolve.

Agility is the name of the game in today's fast paced world and the old rule of...

"If you always do what you have always done then you will always get what you have always got"

Is the biggest load of nonsense ever.

Staying open minded to change, learning new skills and building on previous successes is a proven model.

Quite simply - never stand still.

8

Nothing happens unless YOU make it happen!

It is time to stop wishing, waiting and hoping for your success, and now is the perfect moment to take control of your destiny, and carve the future you know you want.

Learn the skills, take the risks, experiment and learn fast.

Success is created from doing the basics, to a high standard, consistently.

"If a job needs doing you are best to give it to a busy person"

The worst thing you can have is too much time to think about stuff.

I mean, think about it.... what does thinking about it achieve?

Quite often you spend more of your life "thinking about" doing stuff than actually doing stuff.

It's like spinning on the spot. You get exhausted, kinda dizzy but still end up in exactly the same spot.

Choose your tasks and make it happen! Because everything that happens is accountable to you.

Oh, and if you were one of my private clients and spent too much time faffing.

My professional advice would be to STOP Effing about!

10

Your business is your vehicle to do all the things that you want to do with your life!

Please never lose sight of that.

If you cannot enjoy the journey then the destination is irrelevant.

Build the business to give you the life that you want, to do the things that you want and be with the people that you want.

And when given the choice of the hard way or the easy way, then pick the way that brings the biggest results and is the most enjoyable.

I know I would like to be able to quote the legend Frank Sinatra, and say

"I did it my way"

11

You cannot consistently achieve what you fail to believe.

Every action, encounter and conversation you are part of is FULL of possibility and it is almost impossible to capture it all.

Achieving it all is like collecting every golden ticket in the "Crystal Dome" (let's see who gets my analogy) - it is virtually impossible but worth shooting for anyway.

From today onwards consider everything you do and find a way to do it better, achieve a little more and achieve a little more than you did previously.

If you count the moments you will do ok. If you make the moments count you will do more than you ever dreamed of!

Opportunity never knocks on a bolted door.

It steps inside when it is welcomed and encouraged.

Please don't shut the door on people, please don't give up on others and please don't ever think that something is over.

No only means no not right now.

Please be patient. Keep moving forward and keep focussed on your stuff. Keep record of your "No not today's" and be there for them when they are ready.

_13_

Success is the progressive realisation of worthwhile, predetermined and challenging goals.

Dream it, design it, feel it, believe it and then JEDI!

Given the choice of picking good, better or best - which one would you pick?

Most people look to be the best and spend their lifetime failing to achieve that goal.

It is the ones that continually choose to be better that typically go on to achieve more than they once believed was possible.

Stop looking to be your best and just work on being better. Continue this process as often as you clean your teeth and the compound effect of your growth will overwhelm you with pride - maybe not today, but one day...

15

Before ever taking an action or agreeing to do something then please ask yourself "what is the point of me doing this thing?"

Make sure the effort is worth the reward, the outcome can exceed the input and the destination is worth the journey.

Always act think and move...
On purpose.

Be sure to start with the end in mind and always be choosing your actions with the focus on the result you wish for.

17

Nothing happens unless you make it happen...

You are fully responsible for all your success in life and by taking control of your thoughts and actions you can take control of many of your outcomes.

You cannot control everything that happens and cannot control what others think, act or do.

You can control what YOU think, act and do....

That alone is enough to change your world.

18

As the amazing Peter Parker said, "With great power comes great responsibility."

Please never underestimate the influence you can have over other people.

Your actions, beliefs and results are being watched by others and your decisions impact hugely on the world around you.

19

Good is good enough... It's easy to have perfection paralysis and only allow things to be complete when they are just so.

Progress beats perfect and just getting something done and keep moving forward gets you closer to your goal!

_20_

Never finish the day until it is finished on paper.

Write up your activities, reschedule your tasks and sleep a little sweeter knowing all you have achieved and what you have planned next.

21

The creation of good habits and routines allows you the freedom to bring your excellence.

So many people spend their lives chasing their tails and spinning on the spot.

If you fail to lead yourself then you will fail to lead a day, a month or lead an army.

Eliminate unnecessary decisions, distractions and thoughts and use structure and routine to create freedom within fences.

The imagination is a powerful tool and can serve us for every purpose.

It serves for opportunity and demise, love and hate, success and failure.

Understand the power of imagination and use it to assist your journey and just imagine the help you can inspire in others as you help them discover the best version of themselves.

A lesson in leadership. It is not about showing the way to others but lighting the way so others to see for themselves.

The road to greatness is a journey of abundance, accompaniment and companionship.

Take the time to open the doors, create the vision and set light the fire in the people around you. Success is a journey best served in style...

Achieving the desired outcome is only worth celebrating if you have others to join the party.

Measure in moments and not time. Make the moments memorable.

Remember the good ones, learn from the others.

Above all else, keep moving forwards.

You deserve to be your best! To be your best you must try YOUR best!

Stop looking at what others are achieving.

Keep filling your mind with positive beliefs.

Start attempting the things you know you should be doing.

Above all else - understand that right now - you probably have the exact results that you deserve.

The road to success is bumpy, full of obstacles and often very very long.

There is rarely a shortcut or a fast track...

The only thing to speed stuff up is to travel downhill where possible, enjoy the time when the wind is behind you and do all that you can to keep moving forward!

27

When you examine the journey you have already completed, you soon realise how far you have already come.

You have a proven track record of success, personal growth and the ability to overcome adversity.

In my life I have had many people stand in my way and tell me that I cannot do something, am stupid or that my plan will not work. I now can look at those same people in their same lives as my life has moved on.

Guess all I am saying is....

Don't let dumb people steal your dreams!!!

28

When searching for answers - try asking a better question.

29

Focus on the future yet work on the "right now."

Take positive daily actions and watch massive success sneak up and bite you on the backside.

If you have achieved massive success already I am certainly not surprised...

What you must realise though is the foundations you have laid are just a springboard to catapult you to your next success.

The #1 rule - in the words of legendary musical geniuses ;) - Don't stop moving .

If you wish to increase your success then increase your rate of decision.

Pace, momentum and speed of action keep you ahead of the pack!

The days of faffing are a thing of the past.

You ain't got no time for dat!!

31

Before looking externally for reasons or excuses as to why things are not going your way.

Be the first to hold up the mirror and check you are doing all that you can.

Your success is YOUR SUCCESS.

Please stop wishing it was easier and keep working at being better.

32

If you want the part then look the part. What the mind perceives it believes. This is a world in which there is no truth.

Perception is reality and the right outward expression helps you express your journey to success.

33

Success in this business has nothing to do with getting people to change or asking others to join your team.

In fact, success does not even come from showing people what the business can do...

Success is only achieved from you demonstrating to others how your plan is a better plan than their existing plan to help them get what they want.

Put simply - although you are responsible for your own success, your success has nothing to do with you - it has everything to do with what others do BECAUSE of you!

Please remember that ANYTHING is possible. The only thing that is impossible is the ability to achieve EVERYTHING.

This means choosing your battles, planning your victories and picking the activities and actions that get you closer to your goals.

Focus within your limitations, play within your possibilities and STOP looking at what everyone else is up to!

Be your own version of brilliant!

35

If you want to change something about the way your life is...

Then change something about the way your life is!

Be the differences you want to see more of!

36

People rarely get paid more than they are worth!

If you want to earn more then be more and do more!!

Making the moments count and using the pockets of time to deliver small high pay off actions can really make all the difference!

37

Never forget that your business is your vehicle to help you achieve all that you want with your life.

Keep living and never lose sight of your purpose.

S mart people soon realise that they cannot do it all by themselves.

Unlocking the power in others and helping them to achieve more than they believed possible will always raise you up.

Seek the knowledge you can learn from others and you will build on their journeys.

39

When you give out good things then good bounces back.

Not always in direct proportion and rarely in the precise moment you expect it to.

Keep giving the good stuff and selflessly giving your best to others and you soon become surrounded by others who give their best to you.

40

Never underestimate the impact of a little success in just one day...

Repeat this consecutively and your 365 tiny successes will result in far more success than one massive moment.

Daily disciplines and compounded professional effort result in you accessing one of the most powerful forces of all. The force of momentum is almost unstoppable!!!

Did you open for business today and make at least 1 sale??

41

Every second of every day is precious. It is wonderful to think that you can spend every moment doing the things you love.

If you did, you wouldn't love those things, those things would just be normal.

Forget normal and become exceptional in all that you do. For taking the choice today to rise above the norm provides you the ability to have even more choices for your future.

But... Focus on the thing you should be doing at the time you should be doing it!

D on't ever chase the money! Chasing the money rarely leads to success and even if it does it never realises happiness.

When you work hard for your customers' needs and not yours, help them get what they want, see things through their eyes... Then the money will come.

Stay focussed on helping others and quite often the money will be the silent applause recognising the value you have delivered for others.

Life brings many choices and picking the right one has huge impact on your outcomes...

Life also throws many challenges at us and many things that happen are cruel, unfair and just really really hard!

So when faced with the choice of doing something the hard way or the easy way then please don't be stubborn enough to pick the hard way!

Life is hard enough as it is!

Pick the downhill slopes when you get the choice too!

Imagine the creation of an opportunity as the opening of a box.

If that box remains open then so much can happen. The contents could escape, be taken or even get damaged.

Closing the box allows you to the build on the results of that opportunity. Success or failure we win every way.

The most important part of our jobs...

Being a "Professional Mind Maker Upper."

Our job as professional network marketers is as easy as ABC (Always be closing) :)

You cannot be who you are not. Be congruent with yourself, be true to your purpose and don't let dumb people steal your dreams.

Judge your success on the results you help others achieve and not the results you achieve for yourself.

Never forget that your ability to create belief in others, share skills with others and help others achieve their goals will feel great!

The only downside is the by product that you may be rewarded handsomely also ;)

Don't ever chase the recognition, certification or the cheque.

Chase the reason, help the people and live your purpose!

People will rarely outperform their own self-image - help them see more and they will be more!

Great leaders help people see themselves as a better version of themselves and inspire belief that they can reach a little higher.

47

People do two things in life...

1. is what they enjoy doing
2. is what they get checked on

As a leader you have two options with this.

1. help them enjoy it more
2. be prepared to check

You need to do both!!!

Sometimes moments present themselves that are unplanned, don't fit into your routine and there is probably something you should be doing instead.

Those things can wait till tomorrow.
Sometimes - the very best place you can be is - in the moment.

Life is a race! It is a race with only one competitor. You are never ahead or behind because you are not comparing to anyone else.

Your solo race means you are always winning and you are always losing. There is no success without failure.

You will always be ahead of others and behind others - But your race is your race. Be at one with yourself and accept that just realising that you are in a race, and competing for the best you can, in the time you have means you are already ahead of the pack.

Forget the pack and think about yourself. You hand out the encouragement, the discipline and the medals to yourself.

Be the finest competitor you can be and know for certain that the key to success in the race of life is to find your rhythm, keep focus on your own finish line and keep moving forward!

Tomorrow is a brand new start line and you get to run the next leg for the first time!

When the going gets tough, the tough stick together!

Build your tribe, create your culture and nurture your community.

These people will be the best to party with and hustle for you when you're challenged.

Nobody did anything all by themselves.

Before you sleep tonight take a few moments to understand the complete BS we spend much of our days telling ourselves. Understand that if you expect or demand honesty from others then you must start by being completely honest with yourself.

At what point in life did it become ok to start telling ourselves we cannot do stuff?

Why is it ok to convince ourselves that we are not good at things?

Who holds the power to help us unlock our potential?

The only way we have historically learned to do anything is through simply giving it a go!

If we only ever did the things we were born capable of doing.... Then what would life really look like?

You may not have yet realised it , but you have a proven track record of success. Since birth you have achieved massive success every year of your life. You have a history of overcoming adversity and achieving the impossible!

Don't ever confuse yourself by telling yourself the nonsense story of I can't!

The only difference between Try and Triumph....

It's the "Umph" !!!!

Get after it tomorrow and make it count!

52

In life there are precious moments and experiences that truly take your breath away. Moments that you can treasure for eternity...

The thing is... Without the ability to share these moments with others then those moments can easily be forgotten.

Hang on to all that is special to you. Take time for the people that you love and remember to tell them how special they are to you.

Every moment shared is special and every moment only happens the once!

Huge love to you all and privileged to share in this journey with you xx

Bonus

My ultimate daily success formula:

    dream

\+   plan

\+   do

\+   fail

\+   learn

\+   review

\+   refine

\+   repeat

    SUCCESS